From Death to Life

A Walk with Christ
through the Easter Season

Rev. Noah J. Casey

To order additional copies of this book, contact:
Xlibris Corporation
1-888-795-4274
www.Xlibris.com
Orders@Xlibris.com
116251

Contents

Introduction 7

Day 1: Instruments 1 and 2 9

Day 2: Instrument 3 11

Day 3: Instrument 4 12

Day 4: Instruments 5 and 6 13

Day 5: Instrument 7 15

Day 6: Instruments 8 and 9 16

Day 7: Instrument 10 17

Day 8: Instruments 11, 12, and 13 18

Day 9: Instrument 14 19

Day 10: Instrument 15 20

Day 11: Instrument 16 21

Day 12: Instrument 17 23

Day 13: Instrument 18 and 19 25

Day 14: Instruments 20 and 21 27

Day 15: Instruments 22 and 23 29

Day 16: Instrument 24 31

Day 17: Instrument 25 32

Day 18: Instrument 26 33

Day 19: Instruments 27 and 28 34

Day 20: Instrument 29 35

Day 21: Instrument 30 36

Day 22: Instrument 31 38

Day 23: Instruments 32 and 33 40

Day 24: Instrument 34 41

Day 25: Instruments 35, 36, 37 and 38 42

Day 26: Instruments 39 and 40 43

Day 27: Instrument 41 45

Day 28: Instruments 42 and 43 47

Day 29: Instruments 44 and 45 48

Day 30: Instruments 46 and 47 50

Day 31: Instruments 48 and 49 51

Day 32: Instruments 50-51 53

Day 33: Instruments 52, 53, 54, and 55 55

Day 34: Instrument 56 57

Day 35: Instrument 56 59

Day 36: Instruments 57 and 58 61

Day 37: Instruments 59 and 60 63

Day 38: Instrument 61 65

Day 39: Instrument 62 68

Day 40: Instrument 63 70

Day 41: Instrument 64 72

Day 42: Instrument 65 73

Day 43: Instruments 66 and 67 75

Day 44: Instrument 68 77

Day 45: Instrument 69 79

Day 46: Instrument 70 81

Day 47: Instrument 71 83

Day 48: Instrument 72 85

Day 49: Instrument 73 87

Day 50: Instrument 74 88

Introduction

There are many fine spiritual books available that offer daily reflections for the seeker. The uniqueness of this small volume lies in its foundation in the *Rule of Saint Benedict* from the fifth century. Benedict found himself seeking a new path, a new way of life in response to the societal ills and decadence of his day. With the Gospel of Jesus as his guide, the young Benedict abandoned Rome and sought the solitude of a place called Subiaco in Italy. As is sometimes the case, others were attracted to his desire for a more balanced, prayerful life. Eventually, this led to the composition of his *Holy Rule* for monastic men and women.

Keeping in mind that early monasticism was a lay movement in the church, men and women for the past 1,500 years have sought the timeless guidance of Benedict's *Rule.* Chapter 4 of the *Rule* is a collection, mostly from sacred scripture, of wisdom sayings. These could be memorized and pondered by anyone who sought the ever-deepening experience of God. They are tools or instruments by which we cultivate a relationship with God, who calls us always to a more abundant life.

In the early Christian church experience, the period following baptism was known as the "mystagogical catechesis," that is, a time for those newly baptized persons to pursue further meaning of the Christian life into which they had just been baptized at the Great Vigil of Easter. For Benedict, the instruments of good words in chapter 4 of the *Holy Rule* are intended to guide the monastic person into an ever-deepening life with God. These instruments have a timeless value and are just as helpful in the twenty-first century as they were in the fifth century. The daily reflections that follow are intended to guide the seeker who journeys from the Resurrection to Pentecost, and do so with the help of the instruments of good works.

Day 1: Instruments 1 and 2

First of all, love the Lord God with your whole heart, your whole soul and all your strength, and love your neighbor as yourself.

Hearing Saint Benedict begin his own list of good works with the greatest commandment, and especially hearing it on Easter Sunday, leads us immediately to see how the presence of the risen Lord Jesus should impact our lives. We celebrate this day as Christ's ultimate victory over sin and death and come to know Him over and over again in the manner in which we love one another. Sounding deceptively simple, we, Christ's disciples, continue the journey away from the empty tomb of our dashed hopes and disappointments now renewed with the vigor of the Lord Jesus risen from the dead.

Our lives of resurrection joy, however, are interspersed with the realities of daily living, wherein the invitation to live the Paschal mystery is challenged by human weakness and even sin. The first two instruments, as Benedict calls them, that we have at our disposal are the two great commandments of love of God and love of neighbor. No better tools in partnership with One whose risen presence abides with us in every way. As he did with his frightened disciples in those first days following the resurrection, he does now with us. Walking through the doors of our fears and apprehension, he continuously greets us with the words "Peace be with you . . . Do not be afraid." If we find ourselves to be reluctant lovers, we have only to remember that we do not love alone. He who first loved us loves through us and we through, with, and in Him. Herein lies our Paschal peace.

Scriptural references:
    Matthew 22:37-39
    Mark 12:30-31
    Luke 10:27

Day 2: Instrument 3

Then the following: you are not to kill.

This instrument lands upon our hearing rather sharply, especially in contrast to the commandments of love of yesterday. To be admonished not to take life the day after we have celebrated the life-giving event of the resurrection jolts us into realities that surround us. Day after day, the media reminds us of the stark reality of human beings cruelly taking the lives of other human beings. One large city newspaper announces each homicide within the city limits, drawing the readers' attention not only to a prose description of the crime, but also to a graphic map locating the precise time and place of the murder. There are a group of citizens who have banded together and who meet at the site of the crime the very next morning to pray for the victim and the perpetrator. By this public witness, these persons hope, in some small way, to counter the tragedy of killing with the healing power of prayer.

It is not enough, obviously, for us simply not to kill. We must map out our own strategies each day as to how we are going to carry out the commandment of love given to us yesterday on Easter Sunday. Imagine a world in which the daily media noted the acts of love and prayer made by the risen Savior's disciples.

Day 3: Instrument 4

Not to commit adultery.

The challenge that exists long before this admonition is the challenge of chastity. Adultery just doesn't happen suddenly. It is the culmination of smaller acts of lust, infidelity, disrespect, and abuse. To live chastely requires of us the nurturing of our capacity to respect one another—that is, to behold one another as the Latin root word *respicere* would remind us. To use a popular phrase, beholding or respecting another means not being "in that person's face." To behold, I must recognize the sacredness that surrounds each person and that, as a fellow human being, I am a guest in that person's sacred space. On the other hand, to behold means not to stand so far off in the distance that I am unable to hear the call of help and invitation to love and unable to see in the eyes of the other a desire for true friendship best secured through our mutual love of Christ.

If we practiced this kind of chastity, adultery would not be a concern.

Day 4: Instruments 5 and 6

You are not to steal nor to covet.

Stealing and coveting result from a lack of appreciation of the gifts I already possess. The compulsive need for more—more material things, more adulation, more food and drink, more sex, more control and power—leads us to the brink of taking what does not belong to us. Some steal because they are hungry, thirsty and generally deprived of the basic necessities of life. As we reflect on the possible culpability of such persons, our reflection needs to include those who have put them in such a destructive position. Others steal not out of deprivation but because of some sickness that causes them to never be satisfied no matter how much they already possess.

The desire for more that leads to stealing arises frequently out of a combination of a lack of trust in God and God's providential care as well as an insatiable need to insulate ourselves from the possibility of any kind of deprivation. Fear of deprivation, real or imagined, lengthens our arms to wrap around the goods of others, clutching them to our own stockpile of possessions. This sin is characterized by a lack of awareness of what we already have, coupled with a lack of gratitude for blessings given to us by God. Some of us are poor by imposition; others remain poor in our glut of possessions. What is at stake for the disciples of Christ is living out an awareness of the gift of eternal life that is given to

each one in baptism. Pondering this gift and the demands of such
a gift might help us to grab less at more things and people, and to
live with greater interior peace and satisfaction.

Scriptural reference: Romans 13:9

Day 5: Instrument 7

You are not to bear false witness.

Because the Lord is "the way, the truth, and the life," we must live as people walking truthfully on the way with our Companion, Christ Jesus, all the way into life eternal. Truthful living calls out of each one of us an honest assessment of each situation and relationship. Lying may arise out of a need to cover up an area of weakness in our own life. Lying will take the heat off for a while. Lying puts the blame on someone else. Lying, in general, creates a false impression about me, usually by destructively maligning another person.

The more this happens, the more complex becomes the web of deceit that we weave for ourselves. Lying a lot can even convince us that we are other than the person God created us to be. The resurrection is a truth that beckons us to live an honest life, a life that rests in the charity of truth, a truth, as we are reminded, that will set our hearts free.

Day 6: Instruments 8 and 9

You must honor everyone and never do to another what you do not want done to yourself.

If the point of departure in our relationships with one another is honor, then it would seem that I will, in fact, do to others only what I would have done to me. If we encounter one another on the journey to the kingdom of God, with honor, we regard one another with respect. Not even Saint Benedict would say that everyone in the monastery had to be "best friends." He would say, however, that honoring one another as people made in the image and likeness of God becomes the foundation for the kind of love that overlooks idiosyncrasies, faults, and shortcomings.

Honoring one another weaves together with doing to others gratefully only if we want health and holiness for ourselves. If we face addictions, poor self-esteem, and anxieties of various kinds, then we may not be clear about what we would of would not want done to us. The love of God leads us to honor ourselves as people who come to know themselves as icons of God's creative power. Honor is an avenue to conversion and, like God's Word, becomes a lamp for our steps and a light on our Paschal path.

Day 7: Instrument 10

Renounce yourself in order to follow Christ.

Once each Lent, the abbot makes a tour of the monks' cells. This inspection is not considered an invasion of one's privacy. Instead, it is an asceticism that opens the monk to change by either renouncing some material possessions or accepting something from the abbot that will be of some benefit. To renounce oneself is not to somehow become invisible. Renunciation is authentic to the degree that is opens us to a deeper relationship with Christ. Renunciation is not an exercise in self-deprecation. It is an act of love that puts God first in our lives and sees all else in the light of our covenant with God. Self-renunciation renounces our selfish desire to be god in favor of loving God in myself and others. (The Easter mystagogical journey is made together with God in the church.)

Day 8: Instruments 11, 12, and 13

Discipline your body . . .
Do not pamper yourself . . . *Love fasting.*

Are we having fun yet? This ascetically unit of three injunctions has the appeal of standing neck-deep in mud on a July day in southern Indiana. How do these practices help us to celebrate the presence of Christ risen from the dead? We might look at it this way. The concept of "less is more" is gaining some popularity in decorating. There is a thin line between tastefully decorated and cluttered. What the spiritual life seeks to promote is "less is more" both spiritually and physically. As we have noted in previous reflections, the physical renunciation must be at the service of spiritual growth. Otherwise, self-discipline and fasting become ends rather that means, and we end up establishing yet another set of false gods. The culture's preoccupation with body image over healthy bodies reflects this new form of idolatry. Disciplines will vary from person to person. Pampering oneself really means to stop making excuses for not walking with Christ on his journey to Jerusalem or Emmaus or both! Fasting is not quite the same as *loving* fasting. I love it only because God loves me, the authentic person, and maybe fasting will be the physical experience of letting go that reinforces the interior letting go.

Day 9: Instrument 14

You must relieve the lot of the poor.

Coming immediately on the heels of self-discipline, the obligation to relieve the plight of the poor joins personal asceticism with the kind of service of brothers and sisters that keeps us from becoming narcissistic. The obligation also launches a series of concrete examples that mirror the core teaching of Christian spirituality proclaimed by Jesus in the Beatitudes. The encounter with God may take place on the mountain. The sheer magnitude of needs can overwhelm us to the point of throwing in the Christian service towel and simply giving up. One phone call, one St. Vincent de Paul home call, one trip with an elderly person to the store relieves the poor one person at a time. Like life, service begins with a first step. Each specific attempt, no matter how large or small, points out the presence of the risen Christ.

Day 10: Instrument 15

Clothe the naked.

Some have the Lenten practice of going through the clothes closet and identifying items that haven't been worn in the last year. Chances are good that those items will go unused in the coming year as well. One place they can go is to St. Vincent de Paul.

Materially clothing the poor is important, and it must be accompanied by clothing those who do not have the clothing of respect, justice, and human rights. Scripture scholar Walter Brueggeman defines justice as "figuring out what belongs to whom and it back to them." The natural place to begin is with physical things, but the ultimate nakedness of our brothers and sisters is the abject exposure the injustices of bigotry, hatred, and generally being dismissed as persons made in the image and likeness of God. Getting rid of leftovers from our clothes closet might be a good beginning for the more radical asceticism of investing in another, especially the poor, with the vesture of human dignity. The glory of the risen Christ covers all men and women in the seamless garment of redemption. We wear it together and should not tear it. This careful and corporate garment requires of us what Saint Benedict calls "mutual obedience"—that is, listening to one another and anticipating one another's needs. This is the meaning of becoming the church.

Day 11: Instrument 16

Visit the sick.

When we have free time, whom do we seek out for companionship? We probably choose to be with friends who have like interests and who do not demand much from us. Knowing one another, we can relax and enjoy one another's company. This kind of experience renews us and strengthens the bonds of friendship.

The call to visit the sick is not what first comes to mind as a leisure activity. That is probably because for the Christian, it is not a leisure activity, nor is it something relegated to our leftover time. Jesus was acutely aware of this in His day. Those who were sick, and especially those who were incurable, were treated as outcasts and even sinners. Contemporary living has a much more sophisticated way of excluding the sick. It is difficult for those who have lost their physical beauty and mental acuity and who face some terminal illness to "fit in." The sick are to be visited precisely because they are a part of life and the community of faith. They just happen to be sick!

Attending Pentecost liturgy some years ago in the former Oakland Cathedral, I was inspired by the diversity of persons in attendance. In the pew directly in front of me were two women seated next to each other. One was dressed very fashionably and wearing a mink stole, while the other was a "bag lady" who was wearing all earthly possessions. The latter had obviously lost some of her motor control and struggled all throughout the liturgy in putting on and removing parts of her clothing. The well-dressed woman consistently helped her pew-mate in a very inconspicuous manner while never losing her place in the liturgy. I saw in this experience a metaphor for the eternal banquet, the experience of which must begin now in this life. Those who find themselves in the transition of illness need to be recognized as much as when they were healthy, if not more. All will have a place at the banquet table in heaven. We must make certain that all have a place here as well both healthy and infirm alike. What defines Easter finery are garments of grace trimmed with love.

Day 12: Instrument 17

Bury the dead.

A few years ago, I participated in the funeral liturgy and burial of a great aunt, and a great lady she was. As the funeral cortege made its way to the cemetery, I was told that the prayers of final commendation would be held in one of the "chapels" of the cemetery mausoleum. Personally, I've never cared much for this option. Leaving behind the remains of a loved one, knowing that some crew will put them in the ground or a niche in the wall, leaves me with a feeling of incompleteness. The chapel was a rather drab and cold place but was convenient for the cold weather providing underroof parking for many cars. When we concluded the ritual and returned to our cars, I was surprised by the short distance everyone drove only to stop again. As it turned out, the grave of my great-aunt was just on the slope across from the mausoleum. Extra charge or not, all those Irish people got out of their cars, walked up the hill, and had a good look into the grave. No one said a word. The silence spoke volumes. In a few short minutes, everyone returned to their cars for the second time and went on to the luncheon. One moral of the story is never get in the way of a bunch of Irish when it comes to burying the dead.

A second more profound point might be that as we have had the privilege of walking with one another through life, so too do we need to accompany one another to the grave and beyond, literally and spiritually. Other than both beginning with the letter "B," birth and burial are both a part of life. In the Christian dispensation, we profess something beyond burial each time we pray the creed. The communion of saints is not a handy concept to help us deal with death. Much more, the communion of saints is precisely what it claims to be—that is, a community of persons, living and dead, baptized into union with Christ, who has once and for all destroyed death and restored life. In Christ, we travel back and forth across the invisible barrier that separates this life from the life to come, and become aware that our communion with those who have gone before us is as strong, if not stronger than ever. Each Eucharist welcomes all the saints, both living and dead, to this world. We all gather around the table of the Lord, noting in faith that we eat and drink ourselves into Christ's death so that we might eat and drink with Him in the kingdom. Burying the dead is one important moment in this continuous experience of birthing, living, and being reborn to eternal life.

Day 13: Instrument 18 and 19

Go to help the troubled,
and console the sorrowing.

Being a family means accepting the entirety of family life, the happy and the sad times, the serene and the troubled times. The Christian family is no different. There is a temptation to consider sorrow and grief as barometers of sickness. After all, who wants to feel bad? Life, however, brings to us all manner of experiences, including times of transition, limitation, change, and death. All these are reminders to us that we are mortal. Linked with the temptation already named is the illusion that what we like and want the most is unending. Jesus's disciples look into the face of reality and see not obstacles, but traces of grace transforming us from despair to hope. Ours is not to avoid the troubled, but to seek them out with the gift of a compassion that is tempered by respect and a love that is nonintrusive. Because God has pitched a tent among us in the person Jesus, making a home for all persons, we in turn make a home of acceptance for those troubled in any way and afford those grieving a place to do so. When Mary of Magdala, grieving the loss of Jesus, went to the tomb, she found in His risen presence a welcome. As we continue our Paschal journey, life will no doubt weave together resurrection joy with the strands of human affliction and sadness. With Mary in the garden, we seek Christ risen from the dead and the comfort that His new life gives to us all. Our mission is to be ready companion for those whose grief causes them to want to give up hope. The Easter consolation we offer one another begins with the acceptance and welcomes the Lord, who Himself stood in the midst of His grieving friends and wept.

Day 14: Instruments 20 and 21

Your way of acting should be different from the world's way; the love of Christ must come before all else.

The themes of renunciation of the ways of the world continue to be coupled with the positive force of Christ's love. This step reflects another scriptural message that reminds us that our citizenship is in heaven. Once baptized, our first allegiance is to the Body of Christ and its manifestation, the church. All else comes after this. Love makes this possible. The love between two human beings alters their views on many things. It is a love that colors decisions, influences behavior, and expands the context for living. The irony is that this same love of God for us that draws us to everlasting life in the kingdom must be put into practice here in this world. Our renunciation of this world's ways is not a rude dismissal in order to be different. Renunciation only has meaning if it is motivated by the love of God that calls us to greater awareness of our discipleship. In those first days following the resurrection leading to the Pentecost, the risen Lord taught the disciples that He would remain in the world, but in a new way. The early church took its cue from the life of Jesus and set about understanding what it meant to continue to be present in this world, but in a new way. Doing so requires us to live in the present with an eye to the future. This allows us to experience the love of God in the love we manifest to one another in our work, our play, our families, and our communities. We don't need to go someplace different to belong to Christ; we need to be different in the place in which we find ourselves. The love of Christ makes this possible.

Day 15: Instruments 22 and 23

You are not to act in anger or nurse a grudge.

The decisions that we make each day are the best when they are made in freedom. The greatest degree of freedom comes from having clarity of purpose born out of our relationship with Christ. As a human emotion, anger is like a warning light on the dashboard of a car. It alerts us to the proximity of something to which we should pay attention. All too frequently, we act on emotions that lie right beneath the surface of our awareness and make faulty decisions unaware of the source of our anger and its possible connectedness to other forgotten or stored-up memories. The ancient desert fathers and mothers would add that naming our demons is half the battle and deprives them of their false power over us. The point isn't to avoid anger. The point is to make anger another part of our continuous conversation with Christ. Only in this relationship can we know the freedom that belongs to all the sons and daughters of God.

One behavior that contributes to our lack of freedom is clinging to old hurts and grudges. This cultivation of past grievances serves only to perpetuate angers, fanning them into resentments and eventually into hatred. Sometimes we cling to them for so long that they seem life neighbors in our hearts, close and familiar. The false comfort of familiarity might lead us to actually choose lingering low-grade resentment over the release from slavery to the past. Jesus continually encountered resistance to His preaching of a new way of living when He preached to those whose ears could only hear about the possible freedom from Roman oppression. The Lord was trying to get His listeners to hear differently and to see differently. It was clinging to old memories that caused Judas to turn away from Christ and seek a short-term solution for setting Israel free. The spiritual network of grace that is afforded us in the life of the church, sacraments, liturgical and personal prayers, and charity all work together to help us let go of anger, to nurture not the things of death but the things of life.

Day 16: Instrument 24

Rid your heart of deceit.

Duplicity takes energy. To store up and save all manner of half-truths, false impressions, and lies is work. Sadly, it is not the work of the Spirit. No one wakes up in the morning and declares, "I think I'll be deceitful today!" Maybe past hurts or the need to feel protected against some impending harm lead us to begin building an emotional fort around ourselves, which is understandable. Unfortunately, the stones we collect to build this fortification are a collection of fabricated stories, slightly nuanced slanders, and planted suspicions that corrode the heart rather than strengthen it for loving. John's Gospel reminds us that the truth will set us free. The longer we take to clear out our hearts of the clutter of deceit, the harder it becomes to choose a life that is lived without falsehood. The Paschal mystery celebrating the dying and rising of Jesus challenges us to let go of deceit in favor of living the truth. Clinging to deceit, no matter what the motivation, is simply rearranging the burial cloths in the tomb.

Day 17: Instrument 25

Never give a hollow greeting of peace.

The scene from the Bible that may best illustrate this gesture is the encounter between Jesus and Judas in the garden of Gethsemane. The use of such an intimate gesture to carry out the betrayal of a friend is loathsome. In the film version of *The Name of the Rose*, we find a monk whose good zeal has turned sour with jealousy. In an effort to ward off potential thieves and a few of his confreres, he secretly poisoned the top of each page of the sought-after illuminated manuscript. Each time the reader would turn the page—or worse yet, lick his finger to turn the page—the poison would invade his system and lead to death. Offering a false peace to someone is like lacing our warm greeting with the poison of evil intent. The need for the beautiful gift of true peace must arise from a clean heart and good zeal. The life of the church gives us many opportunities for offering, promoting, and nurturing the gift of peace. Our world certainly does not need any more falsehood. What we offer to one another is the peace that comes from God and returns to God. It is a peace that comes to us from our honest encounter with Christ in prayer.

Day 18: Instrument 26

Never turn away when someone needs your love.

Recently, I preached a parish mission and, one evening, spoke about the need for us to be the church that is sent into the world. I noted that the quality of our liturgical prayer, of our eating and drinking the body and blood of the Lord, was an action that needed to extend beyond the comfortable confines of the church building. The poor and the alienated were outside waiting for us to offer them some form of sustenance just as we had been fed at the table of the Lord. While I was greeting parishioners afterward, a man approached me and asked for some help. His clothes were unwashed, as was he. He smelled bad. It was winter, and he was barefooted. He was asking for food. I'm not sure if the parishioners had taken me seriously, but God certainly did. God is very accommodating in that way, and quick too! As we gathered food together for this man, some were filling a bag for him that included things that needed a can opener, a stove, various electrical appliances, etc. The challenge became how to give this man something to eat that was "poor-person friendly," when it is accurate as well as generous.

Day 19: Instruments 27 and 28

Bind yourself to no oath lest I prove false,
but speak the truth with heart and tongue.

One of the greatest sources of human pain is the broken promise. Fractured relationships are frequently so because of a promise that was not kept and quite possibly should never have been made in the first place. How many times have you found yourself hurrying to get someplace only to be stopped by someone who needs to talk with you? Frustrated interiorly, but wanting to be accommodating, you respond "Sure" and then endure the encounter in a distracted, unfriendly, and preoccupied manner. If we could have responded at the outset by saying "I can't talk now, but can I call you?" or "I have about five minutes that I am happy to give you now, let's talk," how much greater the conversation would have been because of speaking the truth. I know one priest who, when asked if he would pray for someone, responds, "Yes, let's do it now." This always comes as a surprise to the one making the request, but the priest knows that if he promises to pray for someone or some intention, he may well forget before he gets around to doing it. Why not do it now? When our truth is immediate in our hearts, it will be immediate on our tongues.

Day 20: Instrument 29

Do not repay one bad turn with another.

This is a classic example of "one thing leads to another." Someone makes a joke about you. You make a little joke about them in return. Pleasant, if feigned laughter. The first speaker will come back with something slightly more piercing, only to receive another barb in return. Polite laughter is much shorter. Before you know it, there is full-scale interpersonal warfare. After you part and go your separate ways, we wonder, how did all that happen? The situation is much more volatile when the encounter is between world leaders who represent countries that both have the capacity for nuclear warfare. You bomb us, we're bombing you. The need for revenge usually arises out of hurt pride. Someone has used us, abused us, or slighted us in such a way we want to "get back" at them. Evil always begets evil. Grace always begets grace. Evil may be nipped in the bud by graciousness. It isn't enough for us to say to ourselves, "I need to shut up" or "I'll just swallow that one." Once again, truth may be the greatest response and the honest way of letting another person know how hurtful his or her comments or behaviors were. This is very challenging when the encounter is between nations. The greatest antidote to repaying evil with evil is to cultivate grace. It may not change the heart of the other person, but it will keep your heart clear of the debris of revenge.

Day 21: Instrument 30

Do not injure anyone, but bear injuries patiently.

"This isn't any fun, and it certainly isn't very satisfying. Sometimes I think a good knock upside the head with a ball bat would be more effective and efficient in bringing about needed change."

In our calmer moments, we know this is not true, and yet, it would give a lot more immediate satisfaction. Being a Paschal person, however, calls us to have a longer vision, a vision that sees beyond the confusion of the early days after the resurrection when the disciples were still hiding under the last-supper table, hoping to be forgotten by anyone who had seen them distributing palm branches a little over a week before in Jerusalem. This injunction not to injure while bearing injuries is not easy, but it is an essential part of learning what it means to be a community, whether it's one into which we are born or one we choose by way of discipleship. The bump and grind of trying to get along unfortunately leads us to injure one another by misspoken words or outright meanness. Admittedly, there are times when we are simply a rash on the body of the community. The rash spreads by sin and is aggravated by human weakness. It needs the healing ointment of compassion and patience. The thing about patience is that it is a two-sided coin. We usually pray for patience with others, the kind of "suffering with" another that helps us to bear one another's burdens. On the other hand, we need to have patience with ourselves, to cultivate the capacity to suffer with our own shortcomings. Patience in our own heart spills over into patience with those around us. Injuring one another decreases as we turn our energies for hurting into energies for bearing with one another.

Day 22: Instrument 31

Love your enemies.

I would rather not. I would either like to avoid them or get rid of them once and for all. But love them? Jesus has this knack for setting the standard for living at an all-time new high. He does so by occasionally slipping terse, direct statements like "Love your enemies." It is so profound that the significance of this little statement doesn't hit us until we start thinking about people we do not like.

How are enemies made? We do not come out of the womb with enemies. We are not given a list in the first grade of those we are henceforth to call enemies. So how do they come about? I suspect that most enemies come about by coming into conflict with our deeply held values. It begins as a simple disagreement and develops into mistrust and disrespect, and before you know it, entire nations are waving nuclear warheads at one another.

Loving one's enemies begins with seeking out those points we share in common, not least of which is our common humanity. Before we know one another's color, ethnic background, language, or political ideology, we all have been made by the dust of this earth into which the Spirit of God has breathed life. This is no common denominator. We all bleed when physically injured. We all bleed emotionally when our feelings have been run over by greed, selfishness, and pride. We all look very dead when we lie in our coffins. Before we get to that particular transition from life to life eternal, we need to seek out those aspects of our life together that we share. We can be companions on the human journey or bullies. Companionship is the much happier alternative. The grace of God mingles imperceptibility with the mead of our desire. With this we can begin to love our enemies.

Day 23: Instruments 32 and 33

If people curse you, do not curse them back, but bless them instead. Endure persecution for the sake of justice.

Apparently the Lord never had to get in and out of a Target department store parking lot on a Saturday afternoon. Cursing has become a way of life. It's easy and quick and lets off a lot of steam. After it's over, we say to ourselves, "I didn't really mean it." Curses arise from a heart that is cluttered with the leftovers of anger's supper. Dining on the junk food of resentment and unresolved bitterness gives us the ultimate heartburn that erupts into curses. Cursing one another never gets to the real problem. It merely displaces pain. Sadly, cursing moves beyond parking lots and bounces back into families and ricochets off national borders.

The antidote to cursing is blessing. Blessings grow in the garden of a heart that is free of clutter. Life's task is to become gracious and for us to be a blessing one for another and not a curse. Only graciousness endures persecution. Heroes likes Dag Hammarsköjld; Dietrich Bonhoeffer; Maximilian Kolbe; the OFM Conv; Mahatma Gandhi; Dorothy Day and Irene Gantz (personal friend); the grateful healed leper of the Gospel; Brother Gregory Loos, OSB; Frances Niehaus (mother and cook); and a host of others who walk with us and gives us good example being not curses, but blessings. In this, they show us a just way of living.

Day 24: Instrument 34

You must not be proud.

A great preoccupation of people today is trying to become someone else. Some go into beauty salons armed with the picture of a favorite celebrity and expect the beautician to perform something akin to the parting of the Red Sea. Others have parts of themselves suctioned out, tucked, lifted, colored, streaked, pierced, or otherwise modified. To enhance who we are is one thing; to attempt becoming someone we are not is quite another. Pride arises out of a highly inflated notion of ourselves of a denial of who we are. God spends our entire lifetime trying to convince us of our goodness, the same goodness seen in us when we were created. Sometimes we believe God; other times we do not.

When Christ left the confines of the tomb, he moved about the countryside as Jesus the Lord, risen from the dead. The light of life pierced every nook and cranny of our self-deception, beckoning us out of shame's shadows into the light of our true identity. Of this we can honestly be proud. It is a pride born out of self-discovery and self-acceptance. In prayer, we discover and accept what God has known all along, that each of us is made in God's image and likeness. This is only truthful reason for being proud.

Day 25: Instruments 35, 36, 37 and 38

(You must not be) given to wine.
Refrain from too much eating or sleeping,
and from laziness.

More is not necessarily better. A friend of mine promotes the concept of "noble simplicity" instead. What do you suppose we are looking for in excess? Perhaps we are looking for something that will, once and for all, complete our incompleteness, fill in the cracks of our existence, and smooth over the road bumps of life. Our desire to be satisfied is certainly human. How we choose to seek that satisfaction is the issue. Food, things, drink, sleep or lack of it, working too much or not enough, snorting and shooting up are all ways of seeking comfort for the realization that nothing in this life will bring us the ultimate satisfaction for which we long. At the point we meet excess, we have the choice to cover it over or fill it up or otherwise deny our emptiness or seek Christ. One approach in prayer is to ask the Lord to take away from us our emptiness. The void we sometimes feel is not an indication that something is wrong. It is instead an occasion to avoid filling it up with stuff that does not last. Only Christ Jesus lasts. Only by standing with Him in our emptiness will we know a friendship that endures into the authentic fullness of the kingdom for which we are all destined in faith. As we continue on our Paschal journey, we need to recall that the tomb is empty in order that our hearts might be filled to overflowing.

Day 26: Instruments 39 and 40

Do not grumble, not to speak ill of other.
Place your hope in God.

From what part of our crabby consciousness does speaking ill of other arise? Somehow, I doubt if it starts from malevolence on our part. No one rises in the morning, stretches, scratches, and declares, "I think I'll be a burr in someone's saddle today" or "I can't wait to get out there and verbally abuse someone." Just now, as I am writing this, a beautiful cardinal has perched nearby, and we have been engaged in a whistling dialogue. (It's the state bird of Indiana, and he has come to greet me, no doubt.) Possibly speaking ill of one another arises when we have not been in a dialogue with creation—that is, when we have stopped listening to the voice of God, who never speaks ill of us, and turned inward to be bored by an attempted dialogue with ourselves. The result is grumbling. I also liked an earlier translation of that used the word "murmuring." One had to distort the muscles of the face just to enunciate the word "murmuring." It distorts our perspective certainly. In His postresurrection appearance, Jesus frequently began the exchange with the disciples, saying, "Peace be with you." That peace arose from His victory over sin and death and all the stuff that fills our hearts like fear, disappointment, envy, jealousy, hurt, and endless comparisons to others. Placing one's hope in God is manifested each time we let our speaking about and conversations with others step out of the tomb of human weakness into the light of Christ, the New Day. Placing one's hope in Christ lifts us out of the morass of our feelings, real as they are, and moves us to trust in the dialogue with God in the risen Christ that always and forever begins with peace. There really is no two-person conversation. All conversations are three-way encounters that include the Spirit of Jesus. Without that Spirit, we run the risk of suffering spiritual boredom and speaking ill of others.

Day 27: Instrument 41

Place your hope in God alone.

The key word in this particular tool of good work is "alone." A monastic confrere once declared factitiously to me that he was sure he could live the ascetical life of the desert monastics, provided he had an outlet to plug in his stereo. It is always easier to place one's hope in God when one is in good health, modestly successful, well-liked, and reasonably attractive, has not missed too many meals, and can easily name friends who think—at least some of the time—that you hung the moon. Placing one's hope in God *alone* is always more challenging and even sometimes painful when we are, in fact, alone. When a spouse stands alone at the open coffin after the others have left, staring down into the mortal remains of a partner taken suddenly away; when you stand alone in a conviction about justice and peace and know the opposition and ridicule of everyone else around you; when you sit alone in your car having just left the doctor's office, where you were informed of a terminal illness; when you wake up in the night feeling totally alone and unable to think of one person who honestly cares about you, then, in those moments, trusting in God alone is hard.

We must practice being alone together, especially in the so-called "good times." The mystery of the Lord's incarnation reminds us that grace is given, received, and practiced in this human world of ours. It is hard to convince someone of the love of God when he or she has not experienced the love of another human being. Maybe this is why Christ insisted on linking the love of God and the love of neighbor and teaching that one cannot say she loves God yet hates her neighbor. At some point, faith demands that I alone place my hand in the hand of Christ, the faithful companion. We must invite Him into our aloneness. It is that presence that transforms loneliness into solitude, providing us a relationship within which we give expression to our isolation, our forgotteness, and our stark awareness that only in God will our souls be at rest; in Christ comes the hope of our salvation. Christ alone is our strength, our fortress, our deliverer (Psalm).

Day 28: Instruments 42 and 43

If you notice something good in yourself,
give credit to God, not to yourself,
but be certain that the evil you commit is always
your own and yours to acknowledge.

When we sing the hymn "Amazing Grace," we remember that what makes grace amazing is God. Grace is goodness, and goodness is not the result of a spiritual recipe, nor is it the reward we earn because we have colored inside the moral lines. Goodness spills over from the eternal source, God, much the same as popcorn explodes and tumbles over the sides of the kettle. However, with God, there is no end to the goodness.

The ultimate manifestation of poverty is the realization that we have nothing. We ultimately own nothing. Nothing we have is of our making, and nothing we do will make what we have and who we are last. All comes from God. All returns to God. We did not arrive in the world with hidden pockets, nor do our coffins have lots of room for our achievements. We are all stewards of God's goodness expressed in countless talents, gifts, and abilities given to each of us. Like the gentlemen in the Gospel, we have a choice to do something with those gifts or bury them in a tin can in the backyard. The motivation to be a good steward is remembering that our goodness is a manifestation of God. Sin is the manifestation of a pride that began by saying, "I can do it all myself."

Day 29: Instruments 44 and 45

Live in fear of judgment day,
and have a great horror of hell.

If one were looking for a statement that might be called "countercultural," look no further. When was the last time you heard either of the phrases "judgment day" or "horror of hell"? The second phrase sounds like the title of a Stephen King movie. The having been said, it is curious that there is some fascination with the idea of "hell" manifested in the great number of novels that give the concept of hell a certain prominence, not to mention the Hollywood versions of demons, devils, and fantastic things exploding from the bowels of cinematic hell.

Even with these preoccupations, it is easy for us to do a little dance around the reality that someday this will end, the new world in Christ will begin, and the transition will be the experience of acknowledging good and evil in our lives. Hollywood aside, what gives us pause to consider the quality of Gospel living is being without God and God's love. That is hell. The fear or awesomeness of our transition into the kingdom of God arises out of an awareness of being without love. Sadly, we experience this absence even now in unparalleled violence, genocide, abortion, euthanasia, and a variety of sadly creative ways we have of being mean. Being without love in the cruel words we speak and in our gestures of petty pride are but spilt-second clips of being without love forever. This awareness might prod us to rely on God who is love to change our hearts now.

Day 30: Instruments 46 and 47

Yearn for everlasting with holy desire. Day by day remind yourself that you are going to die.

My abbot is fond of saying, "I love death." He is the only person in my entire life who has made that declaration. In fact, it is not in the moment of death or the means of dying that one can love as much as it is the promise of eternal life that gives the Christian courage to see beyond. Christians, intoxicated with the love of God that bridges this world and the next, are the only fools, by this world's standards, to speak of death in hopeful terms and to do so with smiles on their faces.

The key word in the first sentence is "yearn." That imperative sets a tone for how we are to live each day. To lean into eternity now mitigates the apparent finality of death. Everything and everyone dies. Nature dies, in some form or another, every day as a way of reminding us that this world isn't the end. This world is the front porch to the very large house of God in which there are many, many rooms. The challenge is to live in this world with an eye on the world to come. The more we cultivate in prayer and charity and our yearning for the world to come, the more death will be a door than a doorstop. The Easter journey does not culminate in death but sees death as a passage to life.

Day 31: Instruments 48 and 49

Hour by hour keep careful watch over all you do,
aware that God's gaze is upon you,
wherever you may be.

Maybe you have had the experience in the grocery store or maybe in a shopping mall. Maybe it has happened to you in some other crowded place when you are with your children. You might be in the middle of a conversation when you begin noticing a small person on your dress or trouser leg. Finally, you acknowledge the incessant tugging with the slightly exasperated response, "What?" The child's response is frequently something like "Nothing" or "Look at me, Mommy" as the child does a little twirl and hop. Children want to be noticed, acknowledge, and loved. They like getting our attention with their insights or antics. Most of all, they want to make sure that we haven't forgotten them. As adults we lose that need, becoming more self-reliant.

Still we like to be noticed, recognized, and accepted. What do you suppose our lives would be like if we were constantly aware of God's loving gaze upon us each moment of every day? God watches our comings and goings and providentially companions us. He sets an example of how we might observe ourselves, not in some narcissistic manner, but as persons who live as though we were constantly in love's gaze, because we are. Hour by hour we monitor our lives not as a selfish preoccupation, but to see how our words and deeds reflect the loving relationship with the One who first made us and called us good.

Day 32: Instruments 50-51

As soon as wrongful thoughts come into your heart, dash them against Christ and disclose them to your spiritual mentor.

The problem with this tool of good work is that it short-circuits fun. That's right, fun. It is definitely more fun to muddle around in the muck of our nasty thoughts. Some sin is hurtful and disgusting. Those who make a way of this kind of sinning usually have several psychological issues that perversely make them experience harm as pleasure. Most of us, however, sin and cultivate "wrongful thoughts" because we like them. We get some kind of kick, some kind of payback, for clinging to our nastiness. So the prospect of giving them up is not always a happy one. When was the last time someone excitedly came up to you and said, "Hey, let's get together and change our ways!"

The initial thoughts, though, are not the ultimate problem. Thoughts come, thoughts go, but eventually, like weeds in a garden, the more we cultivate, cling to, and otherwise kick around our wrongful thoughts, the more likely it is that they will become the whole garden. Hate begins as a wrongful thought about someone or some experience. The capacity to destroy life, be abusive, and erupt into rage all begins with wrongful thoughts. This is why the ancient spiritual wisdom of the desert fathers and mothers, building on Saint Paul and repackaged by Saint Benedict, insists with urgency on ditching the wrongful thought immediately and to do so with prayer and to not do it alone. When we attempt to weed the garden of hearts alone, we always end up in trouble. The point is, we don't have to do it alone. Dashing our wrongful thoughts against Christ the Rock invites the Lord into our very thoughts so that together we can move beyond them in peace. Sharing those thoughts with a spiritual director or "soul mate" can be a trial run for telling the Lord. Do not clean the house before the housekeeper arrives. Do not attempt spiritual tidiness without the cleansing and supportive presence of Christ who, as the Gospel seems to indicate, is much more concerned about us using our energies to cultivate the wheat of faith rather than the weeds of nastiness.

Day 33: Instruments 52, 53, 54, and 55

To guard one's tongue against evil and depraved speech, not to love much talking, not to speak useless words or words that move to laughter, not to love much or boisterous laughter.

Word crafting is an art. We shape our lives by the words we use and celebrate our humanity with expressions of words that lift up meaning for our lives. As with all technological advances, word crafting has been enhanced by the arrival of the computer with all its wonderful connections, linking words together between peoples, their cultures, their sorrows, and their joys. The study of verbal expression has been elevated to that of the doctoral dissertation, not to mention entire university departments. Words are vehicles that are intended to convey thoughts and ideas with systems forging them into communication.

From the moment the infant speaks her first word (a moment everyone awaits with great anticipation) to the moment she will utter her last word before the porch of God's house, that person will have spent a lifetime using words to improve, to communicate, to assist others, to make the world better. Sadly, words also inflict hurt, and sometimes on those we love the most. The words of negotiators, world leaders, spouses, supervisors, employees, teachers, and students are measured and analyzed.

Words matter. God has spoken the ultimate Word in the person of His Son, the Word made flesh. This saving Word has been planted within our hearts, finding a home sometimes amid the clutter of other words and sometimes within a home of the heart made clean by simple, humble prayer. The more we expose ourselves to this saving Word, the more we will see the meaning in all the other words stored up in our vault of expression. Endless chatter, thoughtless or even rude speech, and the noise of superficiality all tear away at the tapestry of honest communication and relationships. Clearly, Saint Benedict is not some ogre always throwing a wet blanket over the party of life. He does, however, seek a word that radiates from a heart that has made a resting place for the Word.

Day 34: Instrument 56

Listen readily to holy reading.

Healing. Instruction. Focus. Frequent, persevering, and uninterrupted prayer.

Whatever else we lack in our society, we do not want for stimuli. No human appetite goes without some degree of teasing, coaxing, or satiation. Whether or not we want it, a ceaseless round of jolts runs through our lives like a person late for a date, driving through rush hour traffic.

Benedict insists, as he did in the very first word of the entire *Rule*, to listen in general and to listen to holy reading. For Benedict, that meant primarily reading the sacred scriptures followed by the ancient writers of the church, notably Saint John Cassian, the author who served as a bridge between Eastern and Western monasticism.

From other insights into the *Rule of Saint Benedict*, it appears that the monastic person was to be exposed to as much holy reading as to manual labor. This may at first appear to be a great deal of listening; however, after listening and/or reading 150 Psalms in the course of one week, reading in the refectory, and individual times for Lectio Divina, there could easily be four hours a day.

For those who were illiterate or, for some other reason, unable to read for themselves, someone was appointed to read to them.

Even in Benedict's day, there were things that would distract the monk from the pursuit of holiness. Hence the need and practice to expose oneself to sacred reading especially the scriptures. We have a choice as to what we allow into our conscious reflection. In exposing ourselves to God's Word, we allow the light of love to pierce through the gray mist of our disillusionment, disappointment, and doubt. What we encounter is the person of Jesus whose gaze continually draws our attention and whose unconditional mercy steers us back toward the path of truth. Listening to holy reading means to not listen to other things like the continual chatter of so-called "news" blasted at us literally night and day. The prayer we make, the wisdom for our daily discernment that we seek, begins and ends with listening. It is the attitude of the seeker of holiness.

Day 35: Instrument 56

Devote yourself often to prayer.

We know very little of the actual prayer life of the apostles. We know that they asked for and received instruction on how to pray from the Lord. It is clear that Jesus also provided regular examples of prayer in various forms such as public healing, close intimate prayer with the Father, and moments of Jewish ritual prayer with His disciples. To devote oneself to prayer, then, follows yet one more example offered by Jesus.

This particular exhortation from the *Rule* follows very naturally from the previous exhortation "to listen to holy reading."

After we listen to a little juicy tidbit of gossip, we practically burst at the seams until we can share it with that "one trusted friend" who, of course, shares it with his ten closest friends. Before long, you may find it on the next CNN Headline News! Why is it that we are devoted to spreading bad news faster than the good news of the Gospel? In part, I suspect we don't have any real stake in most of the bad news we circulate. To devote oneself to prayer means that we have allowed ourselves some degree of vulnerability to the Word of God. Devoting oneself to prayer really means devoting oneself to the person of Jesus. Devoting ourselves to prayer means that we take seriously the relationship of redeeming grace that we renewed in the Easter Vigil.

The devotion arises not just because we have put this in a spiritual to-do list, but also rather because we have allowed the love of God to touch us at the core, even if in some seemingly small way. The point is that we have been touched, and this encounter with the Holy sends us back into that redemptive dialogue with God that we call prayer.

Day 36: Instruments 57 and 58

Every day with tears and sighs confess your past sins to God in prayer, and change from these evil ways in the future.

Confess and change. One of the basic teachings of Jesus's teaching was His insistence upon linking the two great commandments, love of God and love of neighbor. One informs the other. One inspires the other. One gives credibility to the intended relationship with the other. Simply, they are inseparable.

One might think of verses 57 and 58 of the *Rule* in much the same way—that is, you cannot have one without the other. In fact, not only does the exhortation "confess and change" parallel the two great commandments of love, but these verses—57 and 58—also deal with our failure to love God and one another. Sin is the rejection of God and, more likely than not, the rejection of another person.

Confessing one's sins leads to the possibility of change. Not recognizing and claiming one's sinfulness is like a person who goes to the doctor but will not expose her wound for the first step of healing. Worst still is the wounded person who either recognizes no wound or denies that he is even wounded.

Confession of sin necessarily leads to a forgiving process. Returning over and over again to one's sin is useless. It is as if we hear Christ's call to move on yet let our focus slip into the past, unbelieving or unaccepting of God's ready mercy. Fear of the unknown spiritual health can find us mired in the mud of mistakes, clinging to the unhealthy and unholy merely because it is familiar.

Change, on the other hand, calls for risk. It is a risk to leave behind the superficial, quick-fix comfort of our sins and accept Christ's call to an abundant life. This life, this call, expends no energy on the past but rather calls it what it was and moves on.

We are not alone in this endeavor, but we find in Jesus a constant companion who teases out of us our longing beyond sin while fanning the flame of His love, however weakly at times, since it was kindled in us at our baptism.

Clinging to sin and not confessing it is like hauling around a bowling ball all day. Christ calls us to let go of that bowling ball, which might have become a way of life, and walk into the promise of grace with open hands and open hearts.

Day 37: Instruments 59 and 60

Do not gratify the promptings of the flesh,
hate the urgings of self-will."
—*Galatians 5:16*

Why is it that the slightest itch drives us crazy when we are in a situation where scratching is not possible? One of my favorites is in the middle of the Eucharistic prayer. Hands and arms extended, suddenly there is an incredible urge to scratch your nose. It is unlike any itch in the history of liturgical celebrations, and it must be dealt with immediately. Trying not to break stride of the oral prayer as well as not to distract the praying congregation by unusual gestures, you make a quick swipe at your nose. With remarkable dexterity, the itch is addressed, and the liturgy *seems to* continue smoothly; smoothly, that is, until someone casually observes after Mass at the door of the church, "Did you get that fly, Father?"

As much as it may not seem like it, scratching an itch and "satisfying one's promptings of the flesh" are similar, and both are very much a part of being human. Because the situation warrants discretion and reverence, satisfying that the tiny yet preoccupying itch looms as large a problem as any, precisely because of discretion and reverence. The "promptings of the flesh," human as they may be, are sometimes amplified, intensified, and loom larger than life because of the Christian mandate to be chaste. When life is rolling along in reasonably good order and we are living that kind of balance that both celebrates and, in some measure, satisfies our human need for intimacy of friendship as well as the intimacy of solitude with God, the "promptings of the flesh" appear to be under control. However, when life is tipping to one side or another, when the demands of human longing are outweighed by the overload of work, fatigue, and loneliness, our self-will begins bouncing off the walls of our house like a ricocheting bullet, threatening to shoot oneself, the Lord, and anyone else who happens to be in the way and/or looks good.

Balance in life necessarily includes the urgings of our self-will as well as the urgings of the Holy Spirit. Jesus seems to have this in mind when He instructed His zealous disciples about the wheat and the weeds. Cautioning them not to go on a reckless rampage yanking out weeds here and there, Jesus called for patience and serenity, urging the disciples to let the wheat and weeds grow together lest, in destroying the weeds, the wheat is lost as well.

We can certainly pray that the love of God cools the urging of our self-will—be those urgings of power, self-indulgence, sexuality, selfishness or resentment. More important is our prayer that seeks the gifts of patience and peace from God. Those gifts, nurtured by prayer, sacraments, love of God, and neighbor can foster the growth of patience and peace, allowing us to be less preoccupied with the urgings of self-will and more aware of God's presence with us in the midst of all our promptings.

Day 38: Instrument 61

Obey the orders of the abbot unreservedly, even if his conduct—which God forbid—be at odds with what he says. Remember the teachings of the Lord. Do what they say, not what they do.

—Matthew 23:3

Being responsible for one's life is much more demanding than laying the responsibility for ourselves at the feet of another. Sometimes facetiously, other times seriously, we try justifying our activity, or lack thereof, by claiming that the environment made us behave poorly. Hearing this, we roll our eyes as if we have never tried to do the very same thing. How many of us, at least to ourselves if not to others, have claimed that "If only my spouse would change," "If only we had a different abbot," "If only I had a different boss rather than the ogre that presently in charge," and so on, we would be much better persons.

No doubt we must live in the environment where we find ourselves, and sometimes there are goofy things we simply cannot change. However, the serenity we seek comes about by claiming the quality of our response to life and making the best of it. There are days—we all have them—when we simply must choose the best of the imperfect and go with it. If God had fretted about the flawed nature of the cast of characters playing out the mysterious story of the Incarnation, our Savior would never have been born! Several days before Christmas, we endure the proclamation of the lengthy list of who begat whom all the way to the birth of Christ. The point of this is not simply to assure us that Jesus has genealogy. A more important point is to remind us that Jesus came about His flesh and blood honestly and humanly and that His family tree had more than a few twisted limbs. Never once did Jesus blame His anger, His lack of successful preaching, or the fact that among those ten lepers He cured, only one returned to say "Thanks" on His weird family background, His disciples who regularly missed the point of His preaching, teaching, curing, eating with sinners, hanging out with cheats and prostitutes as well as nice folks like Martha, Mary, and Lazarus. In general, Jesus threw around the seed of His Word, nurturing it with unconditional love and hoped that some would fall on good soil.

Obedience is listening to another. Obedience is given readily, not because I like the abbot, the boss, the bishop, or my in-laws. Obedience is given in the monastery because Benedict believed that the abbot stands in the place of Christ. It's not about the other person and his or her personal merits. It's about God. It's always about God. Even in married life, the obedience of one spouse to another is given out of love for God whose love binds spousal love. True, monastic obedience is absolute because the monastic person has given over his or her personal will as a gift to God and the common life. While other types of obedience may not be "absolute," the demand to be attentive and to listen to another calls for a trust that is larger than our own perspective, no matter how intelligent and wise it may be.

Listening—that is to say, obeying—is much easier when get to do the things we like to do. Those occasions are good practice for the times when we must do those things that we would rather not carry out. It demands not mere compliance, but trust. It also places a serious obligation on the ones in charge whose actions, hopefully, will reflect their own trust in God and the desire to listen as well as command.

Day 39: Instrument 62

Do not aspire to be called holy before you really are, but first be holy so that you may be truly called so.

I have tried it. I have tried it many, many times. I have seriously wished to be thinner, and nothing happened. I have, on occasion, wished that my work was done. I concentrated very hard, prayed to Saint Joseph the Worker, and thought wonderful thoughts about the glories of tasks accomplished, and nothing happened. Some spend an inordinate amount of time wishing for many things and never get around to actually doing what it takes to see the task through the end. We sometimes apply this wishful-thinking approach to the spiritual life. While the pastor or parish staff is asking for volunteers to drive nursing home residents to Sunday liturgy, we dream of about how wonderful that would be without ever picking up the telephone and calling to volunteer. Being holy requires us to lift the words of the two great commandments, love of God and love of neighbor, off the pages of the Bible and begin to love. There is no magic fairy dust, no mystical chant, and no verbal or written formulation that makes us holy. As the Gospel observes, some attempt holiness by the sheer multiplication of words. If a few well-placed shouts at God during the General Intercessions at the Sunday Liturgy are good, then regular shouting at God must be better. I have this somewhat profane image of seeing the same cloud that hovered over the Lord in the Jordan River suddenly hovering over our Sunday worship and hearing the same Godly voice speak forcefully form the cloud, "Oh, shut up!"

Holiness cannot be produced out of some kind of spiritual recipe that calls for five pilgrimages to far-off places, hundreds of spiritual one-liners, or even the valiant attempt to rack up spiritual brownie points with our deeds, no matter how good they may be. All that is not bad. All that is, however, the manifestation of holiness and not the source of it. Holiness, like prayer, is God's gift to the person of open heart. As the wonderful chapter 5 in the Dogmatic Constitution on the Church from the Second Vatican Council teaches us, the call to holiness is universal and of God. The task of our discipleship is to receive and respond. Whether or not we end up in a stained glass window or a contemporary icon is not to be our concern. Seeking the gift of holiness from the Holy One and the light of that grace shining transparently through us by the way we live is the challenge and God's glory.

Day 40: Instrument 63

Live by God's commandments every day.

The contemporary understanding of the disorder known as attention deficit disorder has, among other things, offered an explanation as to why certain persons cannot seem to focus. Children diagnosed with ADD, as it is commonly known, find it difficult to stay focused in the classroom or while doing an assignment that requires longer concentration. ADD in adults who where diagnosed in life, even though the disorder was present in childhood, sometimes find it difficult to juggle a number of tasks or to stay focused in a conversation without suddenly interjecting a completely different topic or becoming so distracted by other stimuli that the speaker must repeat herself over and over again.

Staying focused in the spiritual life requires of us all a persistent and concentrated search for God in the midst of our lives. With 24-7 news coverage, constant noise from television, radio, and other entertainment forms, as well as a host of opportunities from which we might choose our activities each day, it is not surprising that we lose our focus on God even as He stands in the mystery of the Incarnation in the midst of our lives.

Living by God's commandments every day, while sounding like a spiritual sound bite, helps in staying focused on God. The commandments of love of God and neighbor keep calling us to return to the practice of loving and its centrality in our receiving and responding to the gift of discipleship. Loving gives us a focus that guides, comments on, and illuminates the various fragments of our lives. In doing so, we may be called to let some fragments drop and select others that will aid us in asking the simple yet profound question of discernment, what will bring me closer to God?

Day 41: Instrument 64

Treasure chastity.

As Benedict elaborates on the previously stated "instrument" about observing daily God's commandments, he offers a listing of dos and don'ts regarding our behavior. The wise abbot begins the list with the invitation to "treasure chastity." If we understand that everything we have and are has come from God and will return to God as gift, then we may understand that we are stewards of all those gifts given to us by God. Sexuality is certainly such a gift. Powerful, energizing, at times a bit wild, and at other times peaceful, the gift of our sexuality calls us to be generative of life in many ways. Chastity is the way in which we nurture and care for our sexuality. All persons are called to chastity whether through marriage, priesthood, religious life, or the committed single life. Without chastity, we may well lose the loving use of our sexuality, leaving it to run rampant or acting like a spoiled child. Using our chastity and sexuality as points of departure in our prayer with God can keep us honest about these gifts and committed to their appropriate use as yet one more powerful way in which we let the love of God shine through us.

Day 42: Instrument 65

Do not harbor hatred.

Hatred is anger gone crazy. Anger is a very human emotion. It gives us a clue to deeper feelings, challenges us to act justly, and provides a focus for new priorities. Anger becomes hatred when we wallow in it like pigs in mud. We may catch ourselves playing with anger either because we don't want to let go of life's hurts or simply because our anger is righteous and intense. Unrecognized and unacknowledged anger can become hatred. Anger must be addressed in conversation with a trusted confidant and certainly with God, especially when our anger is focused on God. Denying or, worse yet, cultivating it is like walking through life with a bowling ball stuck to our fingers. Have you ever tried to hold a knife and fork with a bowling ball in your hand, bless yourself with holy water, and dry the dishes? As ludicrous as that sounds, we do it and wonder why our blood pressure soars.

Anger turned to hatred becomes a toxin in our system, poisoning our desire to love and to be loved. Letting in the Holy Spirit through careful conversation and prayer will have the eventual effect on us that we will pray in the Sequence of Pentecost—that is, the presence of God's renewing Spirit will offer us "grateful coolness in the heat, solace in the midst of woe."

Our hatreds were nailed to the cross with Jesus, and the possibility of growing through our anger became as real as the risen Christ. Anger is part of life and, as such, can become a channel of grace if we open our angered and hurt hearts to God, risking His healing touch.

Day 43: Instruments 66 and 67

***[Harbor no] jealousy of anyone,
and do nothing out of envy.***

One of the greatest temptations we face is to compare ourselves to others. Advertising continually entices us to compare our talents, our bodies, our spirituality, and our way of living to others. In much of this comparing, the message given to us is that we are not "measuring up" to some mysterious higher standard. Comparisons are ready avenues to envy and jealousy. When we are not at home in ourselves, we look to others and try to find our worth in them rather than in ourselves. The goodness that God sees in us, we cannot see because we are so mesmerized by apparent blessings of others. Gradually, we long for the treasures that others seem to have in abundance or desire the gift present in others and absent in ourselves. This longing, this desire removes us further and further from ourselves and the uniqueness of our identity in Christ.

Conversion is not a matter of becoming someone else. Deep, spiritual conversion is a matter of discovering, accepting, and becoming the person God has made us to be in the first place. God spends our lifetime trying to convince us of our innate goodness. Cultivating gratitude fosters a deeper appreciation of God's goodness in us and dismantles jealousy and envy. In fact, with the nurturing of gratitude, we are able to accept ourselves in all our wonder as well as take delight in the gifts of others. It is helpful to take Psalm 136, praying through the marvels of God's presence woven throughout our salvation history, beckoning us to pray "for God's love endures forever."

With deepening gratitude, we can write our own psalm verses of the myriad of ways in which God moves in and among us, leading us to perpetuate the refrain of gratitude "God's love endures forever."

In the Paschal season, we are grateful for the renewed presence of the risen Christ who continues to meet us on the road of disappointments and joys, who continues to walk through the closed doors of our fear, bringing us peace, who waits for us on the shores of our liturgy with the sacred meal of His own body and blood, all the while sustaining us with the gentle admonition "Do not be afraid." For the fear pierced with Christ's peace, we can be grateful.

Day 44: Instrument 68

Do not love quarreling.

In the monastery, there are two options each day for a "coffee break." These brief respites can be renewing or discouraging. One of the monks used to observe that going into a coffee break, each monk had a choice. He could either sit down with the brethren, enjoying time together, offering support by his mere presence, and maybe a simple, kind word. The alternative was to be like a little dog going from pillar to post, hydrant to bush, never leaving much, but just enough to make everything damp!

There are times when the line between good-natured kidding and being quarrelsome is very thin. Much of it depends on our disposition on any given day. I have sometimes wondered about the verse from Psalm 120, "I am for peace, but when I speak they are for fighting." I have wanted to ask the psalmist, "What exactly did you say?"

One of our challenges is to be at peace with those around us. Community living is a continual experiment in not merely getting along, but even more in confronting our personal demons and one another's demons and doing this together. Another challenge is simply to try to be in the presence of those who are peaceful. That doesn't mean they do not struggle with some of the same issues with which we struggle. It means instead that, beneath the surface of life, they are connected with a life-giving source of serenity that in fact cushions the bumps and grinds of daily living.

The contact with this kind of peace is the serenity that comes through the risen Lord. In many of the postresurrection appearances of Christ, He brings a message of peace. Quarreling grows out of a variety of displaced feelings like anger, mistrust, and hurt. Quarrelsome persons not at home in themselves. An inconsolable child who whines and moans is frequently tired and needs a nap. Adults tire also. Emotional, physical, and spiritual fatigue wear us down, and we find ourselves regularly disquieted and contentious even concerning the most seemingly minor points. There is no energy left to cultivate gratitude. I spend precious energy on words, opinions, and attitudes that irritate my interior spirit and the spirit of those around me.

Easter peace might be found in drawing close to the source of peace, the risen Lord. Standing in the shade of His presence might just bring about healing and be a balm for the anxious heart.

Day 45: Instrument 69

Shun arrogance.

Arrogance is a house made of cards or, biblically speaking, a house built on sand. Guaranteed to eventual failure, arrogance promotes an image that is disconnected from the truth because it projects a false picture of one's self. Associated with, but distinct from pride, arrogance is a mask that frequently covers poor self-esteem, little self-perception, and fear. A cousin to pride, arrogance leads one down a path to greater alienation from others, indeed, from one's true self. Arrogance pushes others away, keeping them at a safe distance. Arrogance is different from self-confidence in that self-confidence is based on fact.

In the monastic school of the Lord's service, the continuous call to conversion applies the solution that strips away the old veneer of self-delusion layer by layer. It is no wonder that monastic men and women vow *conversion of one's manners* for life! The cycle of the liturgical seasons, the continuous efforts to seek balance, the common good, and God serve to wipe away delusions and, once again, discover the beautiful, clean surface of one's true self. All this requires patience on the part of the person in conversion, as well as those with whom he or she prays, plays, and works out the stuff of everyday living.

In the early church, as has now been theoretically been restored, the time after Easter focuses on *mystagogia*, a period of continuing formation and deepening the spiritual life of the recently baptized. In the contemporary times, it is difficult to maintain this level of commitment after the climactic experience of the Easter vigil. No less is the case with shunning arrogance. Even the newly received gift of God's life in baptism can become an arrogant mask unless I regularly stand, spiritually speaking, in the rushing waters of God's new life that, current by current, smooth over the stone of my heart, revealing the Ezekiel-promised stone of flesh.

Day 46: Instrument 70

Respect the elders.

To enter monastic life and suddenly find that one has an instant family of all brothers, most of whom are older, can be quite challenging. To observe from one's place in the guest section in church the monks slowly processing all in the same manner and the same monastic habit and steadily moving toward the same destination is one thing. To live among them, discovering the vast array of idiosyncrasies, unique personalities, and individuals going in all directions is quite another matter. Each day, as the community forms in *statio*, the preparatory lineup for procession, the young monastic walks to his or her place at the head of the line, making the silent journey past community members who have been forming *statio* for many years. Passing by these brothers in community, seeing one who has suffered from poor health over a prolonged period, seeing another whose stooped shoulders reveal years of hard labor or another whose fidelity to choir and the common life offer unassuming perseverance, all serve to encourage the neophyte in monastic life.

One such monk always had the appearance of having just chewed on gravel. Having a face literally drooping, a somewhat severe countenance, and a monotonic voice so seldom heard that one wonders if it was artificial, this elder member of the community appeared aloof and uninterested. Suddenly, as the waning days of Advent gave way to this novice's first monastic Christmas, another side of the older monk was revealed. It seems that years before, he had received the gift of a beautiful Hummel nativity set and had permission to display it at Christmas time. With the door of his cell open, one could see the Hummel nativity set displayed on beautiful material draped over a tall filing cabinet. It remained that way throughout the entire Christmas season, offering an oasis of beauty as community members slowly passed by. Inquiring about this practice of my old confrere, I also discovered that he wrote beautiful poetry that on occasion revealed a subtle and insightful sense of humor. After these experiences, this senior monk no longer seemed foreboding or forbidding to me. I learned him.

In a culture that frequently overlooks the acquired wisdom of its senior citizens and hurries past them like abandoned vehicles along the highway of life, monastic life offers a renewing perspective on living with older members. The word "respect" comes from a Latin word meaning "to behold." One goal of the common life is to provide an experience wherein the same goodness that God beheld in each of us and all creation from the beginning might again encourage youth to behold the senior members of human community, recognizing the goodness of their younger years now highlighted by the acquisition of wisdom that gives younger people hope.

Day 47: Instrument 71

And love the young.

The *Rule of Saint Benedict* makes provisions for youth in a number of instances, including how the young, presumably children, were to be disciplined and taught. Some of these children stayed in the monastery to become fully professed members of the monastic community. Living in a close-knit community is a blessing and can also be challenging. Kids are kids, so to speak, and kids will do the kinds of things that kids do. The structure of the monastic life offered a kindly, clear manner in which relationships between the young and the old, strained at times by the gap in age and the natural tendencies of various age groups, could flourish.

The very structure of monastic life offers a plan for the young and the old to relate, pray, work, eat, and sleep. Such a structure encourages the kind of living that might foster the attitude of love for the younger members. It is the love of the dying and rising of Jesus and sees the fostering of human and spiritual development as an expression of honest, humble love.

For all of us, love is the inspiration and the teacher. Like community life, family life thrives wherein that kind of love for the younger members encourage patience as well as discipline, learning as well as manual labor and respect for the individual as well as the common good. This love looks beyond cultural fads to timeless values that guide and shape our lives. In our own time, the example of love manifested in the midst of our life together in the human community would go a long way to lead youth into maturity.

Day 48: Instrument 72

Pray for your enemies out of love for Christ.

This exhortation may seem a bit strange for a close community of monks sharing a common search for God. At the same time, the close-quartered life of monks can take ordinary dislike between people, and elevate it to the level of being enemies. The issues are not those of ancient ethnic rivalries nor generations of cultural warfare. Enemies within the monastic life gradually develop over time, almost imperceptibly at first, but grow steadily into deeply felt animosities.

The seeds of this animosity are found in narcissism, a self-centered preoccupation with having one's own needs met, rather than focusing on the common good. Other factors that contribute to individuals becoming enemies are unacknowledged hurts that evolve into deeply rooted resentments and allowing adherence to particular ideologies, losing sight of the human beings behind the mask of opinions. The psalmist notes, "How good and how pleasant it is—brothers living in harmony." This harmony of fraternity is never established on fickle human frailty, no matter how intense the desire for harmony. We cannot love our enemies without the inspiration that comes from loving Christ. Any attempt to love one's enemies out of sheer willpower will ultimately fail. Love of enemies as well as love of friends must be founded and focused on Christ's love for us all and our loving desire for Christ. This love and only this love will be strong enough to support or human efforts—sometimes strong, sometimes weak—to love our enemies.

Day 49: Instrument 73

***If you have a dispute with someone,
make peace with him before the sun goes down.***

One time, a certain abbot observed somewhat, that passive-aggression was the glue of monastic life. The guarded laughing response of his monastic confreres acknowledged the note of truthfulness in the statement.

All God's children are called to live in the freedom of God. It is a freedom that springs forth along with the surging waters of baptism. We cultivate this freedom during the Easter season as we witness the power of Christ's liberating resurrection that has once and for all broken the chains of our slavery to sin and death.

Doubt, hurt, pride, and mistrust can foster within us that reluctance to hand over our grudges. We find ourselves clinging to and wallowing in the muck of old disputes. The longer we cling to these, the more difficult it becomes to live in freedom. If we take our grudges and resentments with us, we do not enter into that rest that comes only with humble acceptance and apology. Even if the original dispute was not our fault, or even if our expressed desire for reconciliation is rejected, we must at least let go of bitterness and, with freed hands, hold gently, if steadily, the gift of interior peace that is nurtured by our desire for peace among us.

Day 50: Instrument 74

And finally, never lose hope in God's mercy.

One time while visiting a monastery of Benedictine Sisters, I became acquainted with one of the senior members of the community who had been professed for over sixty years. As a young sister, she had undergone brain surgery, and the procedure had gone badly, leaving her severely disabled for life. Having lived for many years in a very disabled manner, she still came to Eucharist and choir every day. Watching her very deliberate and careful, strained efforts to turn a single page of the prayer book was inspiring.

On one occasion, a benefactor visited the monastery for liturgy and supper. He had been diagnosed just months before with Lou Gehrig's disease. Confined to a wheelchair and living with the steadily decreasing use of his hands and speech, he remained very faith filled and positive, with a striking sense of humor. At the end of the meal, the sister asked to be wheeled alongside the guest. With wide eyes, a big smile, and great conviction, she said, "Ray, I've been praying for you!" She thanked him for his kindness. As I wheeled her to her cell in the infirmary, she said to me with great joy, "This has been a great week!"

This life is not meant to be perfect. Poor health, the sudden death of a loved one, the pain of divorce, societal alienation, and a host of other debilitating experiences can shove us further and further into the depths of despair. The unrelenting press of our own sinfulness can leave us wondering if we will ever make any progress at all in the spiritual life.

Regularly, penitents will express their reluctance to continue to the Sacrament of Reconciliation because they find themselves confessing "the same old sins." The fact is that, while our sins may have the dull familiarity of dirt, we ourselves are never the same. We are always changing, even if we resist that change. More importantly, our temptation to despair will always overwhelm us as long as we forget our relationship with God. For ourselves alone, life is not possible, but *with* God, all things are possible.

Just as the risen Christ pierced through the dense despair of the forlorn disciples fleeing to Emmaus, so too will our acceptance of Christ's companionship, walking along the path of our human journey, diminish our despair and foster our hope.

End Note

The quotations from the *Holy Rule of Saint Benedict* are taken from

Timothy Fry, editor, RB 1980: *The Rule of Saint Benedict in Latin and English with Notes* (English and Latin Edition) by Saint Benedict (Collegeville, Minnesota: Liturgical Press, March 1981).

CPSIA information can be obtained at www.ICGtesting.com
Printed in the USA
LVOW050704280413

331166LV00002B/3/P